Deciduous Forest Animals

Biome Beasts

Lisa Colozza Cocca

Rourke Educational Media

A Division of Carson Dellosa Education

rourkeeducationalmedia.com

BEFORE AND DURING READING ACTIVITIES

Before Reading: *Building Background Knowledge and Vocabulary*

Building background knowledge can help children process new information and build upon what they already know. Before reading a book, it is important to tap into what children already know about the topic. This will help them develop their vocabulary and increase their reading comprehension.

Questions and Activities to Build Background Knowledge:

1. Look at the front cover of the book and read the title. What do you think this book will be about?
2. What do you already know about this topic?
3. Take a book walk and skim the pages. Look at the table of contents, photographs, captions, and bold words. Did these text features give you any information or predictions about what you will read in this book?

Vocabulary: *Vocabulary Is Key to Reading Comprehension*

Use the following directions to prompt a conversation about each word.

- Read the vocabulary words.
- What comes to mind when you see each word?
- What do you think each word means?

Vocabulary Words:
- brush
- burrows
- distinct
- dormant
- hibernate
- migrate
- pellets
- subtropical
- territory
- undercoat

During Reading: *Reading for Meaning and Understanding*

To achieve deep comprehension of a book, children are encouraged to use close reading strategies. During reading, it is important to have children stop and make connections. These connections result in deeper analysis and understanding of a book.

 Close Reading a Text

During reading, have children stop and talk about the following:

- Any confusing parts
- Any unknown words
- Text to text, text to self, text to world connections
- The main idea in each chapter or heading

Encourage children to use context clues to determine the meaning of any unknown words. These strategies will help children learn to analyze the text more thoroughly as they read.

When you are finished reading this book, turn to the next-to-last page for **Text-Dependent Questions** and an **Extension Activity**.

Table of Contents

Biomes

A biome is a large region of Earth with living things that have adapted to the conditions of that region.

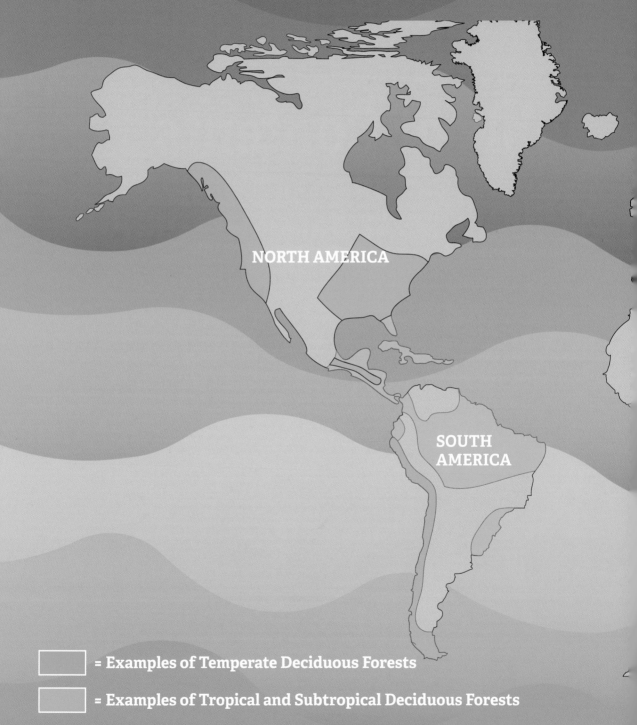

NORTH AMERICA

SOUTH AMERICA

= Examples of Temperate Deciduous Forests

= Examples of Tropical and Subtropical Deciduous Forests

There are two main types of deciduous biomes: temperate deciduous and tropical and **subtropical** deciduous.

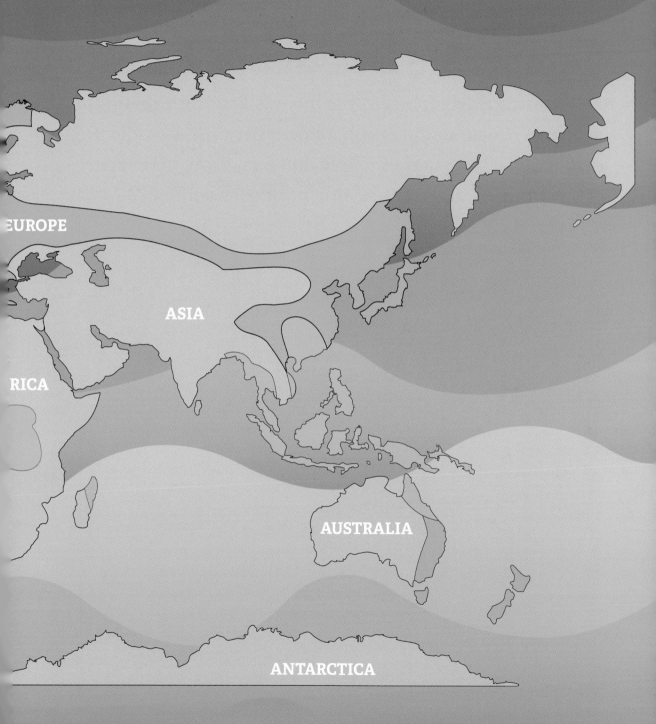

Temperate Deciduous Forests

Temperate deciduous forest biomes have four **distinct** seasons. Precipitation is spread over the year. Broadleaf deciduous trees, such as maple and oak, grow here. Leaves drop in the fall and trees go **dormant** over winter.

The temperate deciduous forest is home to mammals of all sizes. Mice, porcupines, raccoons, bears, and bobcats live here. The white-tailed deer is a common sight. In the spring, deer eat soft grasses and flowers. They adapt their diet in winter and eat bark, twigs, and woody plants.

The eastern chipmunk eats seeds, fruit, and insects. Chipmunks have stretchy cheek pouches. In the summer and fall, they gather food in their cheeks and store it in their **burrows** for winter. In winter, they go into a deep sleep, or *torpor*. They wake often to eat their stored food.

eastern chipmunk

Many birds, such as cardinals, robins, and eagles, live in temperate deciduous forests too.

robin

cardinal

The northern goshawk is a large gray predator bird. It mainly eats rodents, rabbits, and other birds. Its broad, rounded wings help it fly, glide, and swoop down quickly and quietly upon its prey. If food becomes too scarce in the winter, hawks **migrate** south to find food.

Barred owls remain active year-round. They are meat-eaters. These skilled hunters have hearing almost two and a half times as sharp as a person's hearing. They can hear mice squeak from 660 feet (201 meters) away. Barred owls swallow prey whole and spit up **pellets** made of the prey's bones and feathers or fur.

Cold-blooded reptiles and amphibians can also be found in temperate deciduous forests. Copperhead snakes are brown with bands of lighter brown. The coloring blends in with rocks and **brush**.

A copperhead is a pit viper. Pits on both sides of its head are sensors that detect warm spots to help the snake locate nearby prey. In the winter, it slithers into an underground den with other snakes to keep warm.

Did You Know?

The copperhead snake bites more people in the United States than any other snake.

American toads also avoid the cold. They **hibernate** in deep burrows. When winter ends, the toads keep busy eating about 1,000 bugs a day. Their warty skin helps keep predators away. Glands in the skin release poison!

Insects and arachnids also call the temperate deciduous forest home. A cicada digs a deep underground burrow. It uses its sharp, tube-like mouth to cut through plant roots and suck up the sap. Some kinds of cicadas stay underground for a year. Others stay underground for 13 or 17 years.

Did You Know?

Staying underground protects cicadas from predators who forget that the insects are there!

Black widow spiders hide under rocks and leaves. In the winter, they choose between two ways of surviving. Some spiders move into nearby buildings. Others slow their heart and breathing rates, so less energy is needed to survive in the cold.

Tropical and Subtropical Deciduous Forests

Tropical and subtropical forest biomes have a wet and a dry season. Heavy rains fall during the wet season. Little to no rain falls during the dry season. It is warm to hot all year. Teak, palm, and bamboo trees are common here. Leaves drop and trees go dormant during the dry season.

Did You Know?

Sloth bears eat insects. Their nostrils close when they stick their snouts into insect nests and hives. Their two front teeth are missing so they can suck up the bugs.

Mammals in tropical and subtropical deciduous forests adapt to the heat and long dry spells. The sloth bear lives in the forests of South Asia. It has shaggy fur with no **undercoat**. This helps the animal release some of its body heat.

Ring-tailed lemurs live in the hot forests of Madagascar. Lemurs use their hands and feet to move among trees. They spend up to half their day on the ground, where it is cooler. Lemurs eat fruit, plants, and sap. During the dry season, lemurs travel great distances to find food.

peacock

The peacock lifts its long back feathers with its short tail feathers and fans them out. The feathers make it easy for predators to spot the bird. The peacock will run or fly away if frightened. Peacocks are the largest flying birds.

peahen

Did You Know?

The female peahen is much plainer than the peacock. Its brown feathers help it blend in with the shrubs where the nest is hidden.

The black-throated magpie-jay is blue and white with a black throat. This smart bird nests about 100 feet (30 meters) high in a tree so fewer predators can reach it. It hides extra nuts and berries during the wet season. It remembers where the food is hidden and returns when the food is needed.

Did You Know?

The black-throated magpie-jay is a farmer too! Some of the food it hides gets left behind and grows into new plants.

Reptiles and amphibians in tropical and subtropical deciduous forests change their behaviors in each season. During the wet season, the Nile crocodile lives alone in its own **territory** in a river or swamp. The rivers and swamps shrink during the dry season. The crocodiles adapt by living together and sharing whatever water is available.

Did You Know?

Nile crocodiles eat mainly fish, but they will eat anything that crosses their path. About 200 people each year are eaten by Nile crocodiles!

The mountain chicken frog, or giant ditch frog, is one of the largest frogs found in tropical and subtropical forests. During the wet season, it sits and waits for prey to pass by. The frog's coloring helps it blend in with the soil.

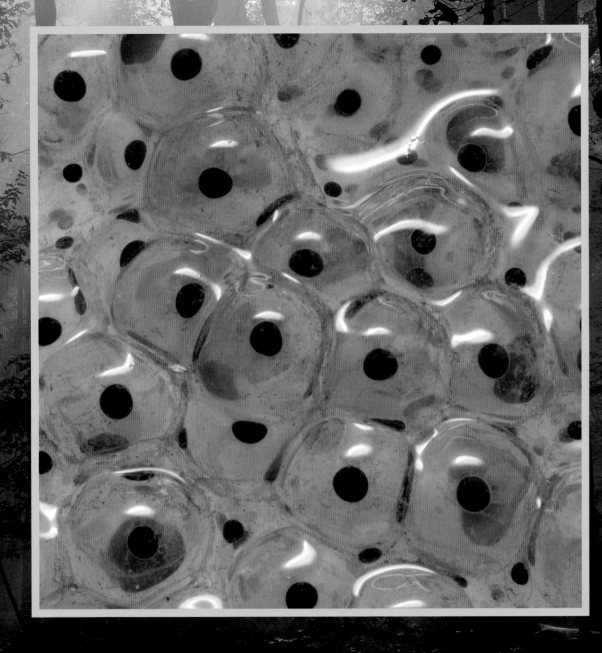

The female has a special adaptation that protects its young during the dry spell. The frog digs a burrow in the soil. Then, she produces a thick foam that forms a nest in the burrow. The foam keeps the eggs and tadpoles moist during the dry season. The female adds foam as needed. The young frogs reach adulthood and leave the burrow when the wet season returns.

Many insects and arachnids live in these wet/dry
forests. The citrus swallowtail butterfly hides easily
among plants. The young caterpillar is dark and glossy
with white markings. It looks like bird droppings on a leaf.
The caterpillar turns all green as it ages and blends in
with the leaves.

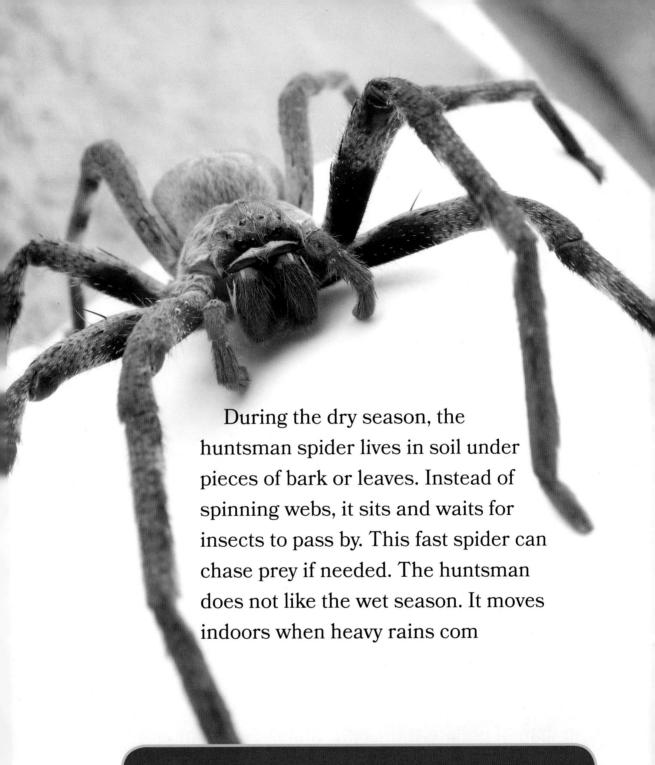

During the dry season, the huntsman spider lives in soil under pieces of bark or leaves. Instead of spinning webs, it sits and waits for insects to pass by. This fast spider can chase prey if needed. The huntsman does not like the wet season. It moves indoors when heavy rains com

Did You Know?

The huntsman spider is sometimes called the giant crab spider. Its long legs spread out like a crab's.

Deciduous forest biomes are filled with life. The plants and animals in these biomes have adapted to the challenges of the climate and learned to survive and thrive in all seasons.

ACTIVITY: Camouflage

Many animals in deciduous forests use camouflage for protection. Learn about camouflage with this project.

Supplies

- two sheets of cardstock
- scissors
- plastic wrap
- tape
- colored pencils
- green construction paper

Directions

1. Cut the center from a sheet of cardstock, creating a frame.
2. Tape plastic wrap over the frame, completely filling in the opening.
3. On a second sheet of cardstock, draw either a temperate deciduous forest in late fall or a tropical deciduous forest in the dry season. Include trees, plants, and animals. Make sure to color each animal correctly and to show it in a place where it actually lives in the forest. Do some research if you need to.
4. Cut leaf shapes from green construction paper. Tape them onto the plastic wrap frame.
5. Cover your forest picture with the frame. Can you see the animals?
6. Slowly remove the leaves from the frame one at a time.

Could you see more animals before or after the leaves were gone? How many leaves were removed before all the animals could be seen? How did each animal's coloring make it easier or harder to see? What kind of camouflage do you think would best help animals living in the biome you chose?

Glossary

brush (bruhsh): land where small bushes grow

burrows (BUR-ohs): holes underground used as animal homes

distinct (di-STINGKT): clearly different from others

dormant (DOR-muhnt): state in which a plant is alive but not growing

hibernate (HYE-bur-nate): a state of long sleep in which an animal's heart and breathing rates slow greatly

migrate (MYE-grate): to move from one region to another at a particular time of the year, especially to find food or water

pellets (PEL-its): small, hard balls of materials that cannot be digested, such as bones and feathers

subtropical (sub-TRAH-pi-kuhl): areas next to hot, wet tropical zones

territory (TER-i-tor-ee): a separate area belonging to an individual or a group

undercoat (uhn-dur-KOHT): a layer of short hair or fur covered by a longer, coarser, or thicker coat

Index

Text-Dependent Questions

1. What does the huntsman spider do when the heavy rains come?

2. Describe how a mountain chicken frog cares for its young.

3. Why are burrows important in both temperate and tropical deciduous forests?

4. Why do you think the author explains how lemurs are different from monkeys?

5. Explain why the camouflage of the caterpillar of the citrus swallowtail butterfly works well.

Extension Activity

Pretend you have a chance to move to either a temperate or a tropical or subtropical deciduous forest. Which would you pick? Why? What adaptations might your family have to make to deal with the challenges of the biome? Write your ideas.

About the Author

Lisa Colozza Cocca has enjoyed reading and learning new things for as long as she can remember. She lives in New Jersey by the coast. One of her life goals is to never meet a copperhead snake while out in the woods. You can learn more about Lisa and her work at www.lisacolozzacocca.com.

www.rourkeeducationalmedia.com

PHOTO CREDITS: Cover & Title Page: © mikespics, ©Patrick_Gijsbers, ©guenterguni; Pg 1, 12, 18, 20, 22, 24, 26, 29, 30, 32 ©AVTG; Pg 1, 3, 6 ©ekolara; Pg 4 ©CarlaNichiata; Pg 6 ©Patrick Foto; Pg 7 ©KenCanning; Pg 8 ©BrianLasenby; Pg 9 ©rpbirdman, ©NightAndDayImages; Pg 10 ©Andyworks; Pg 11 ©suefeldberg; Pg 12 ©Wildvet; Pg 14 ©JasonOndreicka; Pg 15 ©WerksMedia; Pg 16 ©JasonOndreicka; Pg 17 ©Ramdan_Nain; Pg 18 ©Patrick_Gijsbers; Pg 19 ©luobin17; Pg 20 ©wonry; Pg 21 ©shah.jai; Pg 22 ©rkhphoto; Pg 23 ©BirdImages; Pg 24 ©Matthijs Kuijpers; Pg 25 ©Gannet77; Pg 26 ©Timothy Olls; Pg 27 ©Jon Richfield; Pg 28 ©suefeldberg

Edited by: Kim Thompson
Cover design by: Kathy Walsh
Interior design by: Rhea Magaro-Wallace

Library of Congress PCN Data

Deciduous Forest Animals / Lisa Colozza Cocca
(Biome Beasts)
ISBN 978-1-73161-440-7 (hard cover)
ISBN 978-1-73161-235-9 (soft cover)
ISBN 978-1-73161-545-9 (e-Book)
ISBN 978-1-73161-650-0 (ePub)
Library of Congress Control Number: 2019932140

Rourke Educational Media
Printed in the United States of America,
North Mankato, Minnesota